My mom's not around," Rachel said, "and just thinking about her gets me all upset. I wonder why she left and why she won't come see me. . . .

"I used to be afraid to talk to God about my anger, 'cause I figured He didn't approve. But since God knows I feel this way, I might as well tell Him about it. He helps me get the anger out and feel better."

"I'm so glad God understands us," said Anna. "But it's still hard."

About the Authors of This Book

Beth Matthews is the pen name for an eleventh-grade Christian with an adventuresome spirit and contagious smile. She's the kind of person who makes you glad to be alive. She understands blended families from personal experience and the experiences of her friends. She helped create the characters in this book because she knows God is the one who helps us build happy families. God makes daily life an adventure for Beth.

Andrew Adams is the pen name for a tenth-grade Christian who likes to make friends with people of all ages. He likes all kinds of sports and is very committed to God and his church. Andrew lives in a blended family and likes it. He helped create the characters in this book because he wants all kids to live in happy families. Andrew displays a refreshing honesty and a personality that brings positive attention to God.

"Anna," "Brian," "Rachel," and "Ken" are the creations of Beth and Andrew.

Karen Dockrey is a youth minister and writer who likes to study the Bible with teenagers. She's convinced that God has the answers to our questions and that living according to His Word can create happy families, blended or not. She asks God to give her the words and guide her to the actions that will make her home a happy place. She's the author of over twenty books including three others in the KIDS HELPING KIDS series.

Kids Helping Kids
A Christian Approach

I Only See My Dad on Weekends

Kids tell their stories about divorce and blended families

Beth Matthews, Andrew Adams
and **Karen Dockrey**

Chariot Books™
A Division of Cook Communications

Chariot Books™ is an imprint of David C. Cook Publishing Co.
David C. Cook Publishing Co., Elgin, Illinois 60120
David C. Cook Publishing Co., Weston, Ontario
Nova Distribution Ltd., Eastbourne, England

I ONLY SEE MY DAD ON WEEKENDS
© 1994 by Karen Dockrey

Designed by Jeffrey P. Barnes
Cover illustration by Rick Kroninger
First printing, 1994
Printed in the United States of America
98 97 96 95 94   5 4 3 2 1

Library of Congress Cataloging-in-Publication Data

Matthews, Beth.
        I only see my dad on weekends : kids tell their stories about
divorce and blended families / Beth Matthews, Andrew Adams,
and Karen Dockrey.
            p.   cm. — (Kids helping kids)
        ISBN 0-7814-0110-0
        1. Divorce—United States—Psychological aspects—Juvenile
literature. 2. Children of divorced parents—United States—Life
skills guides—Juvenile literature. 3. Stepfamilies—United States—
Juvenile literature. [1. Divorce. 2. Stepfamilies.] I. Adams, Andrew,
1977-   . II. Dockrey, Karen. III. Title. IV. Series.
HQ777.5.M375   1994
306.89—dc20

                                                                94-4733
                                                                    CIP
                                                                     AC

Contents

The Kids Helping Kids Series

You'll Never Believe What They Told Me
Trusting God through serious illness

I Only See My Dad on Weekends
Kids tell their stories of divorce and blended families

Where Can I Find A Real Best Friend?*
Being yourself while being a friend

I'm A Person, Just Like You*
What it's like living with a learning disability

*coming soon

▶ Introductions

Sometimes I wonder if my stepdad and I will ever get along. We hardly say two words to each other. I'd like to talk to him about things, but he's really quiet. Then on days he does talk, he seems to want me to listen and not do any of the talking. If I say anything, he gets quiet again. I'm really not trying to cause a problem; I just want him to know my ideas. I guess we don't have enough in common."

"I think you should keep trying to talk to him," said Brian. "But it's not easy to do. My stepmom and I don't often see eye-to-eye on things."

"It's different in my family," said Rachel. "I can talk to my stepmom real easily; it's my mom I don't get along with. My stepmom and I can argue and still be close. She understands I'm just expressing my opinion, not trying to start World War III."

"Yeah," said Ken. "My stepmom is like a real parent. I can state my opinion and she states hers. Even when we disagree, I treat her like she's right so I can hear her side of the story. We both go away happy."

Are all stepparents big bad meanies? Not at all. As these kids have said, parents are easy or hard to get along with depending on how they choose to treat their kids—and on how the kids choose to treat the parents. Understanding and caring work whether you have two, three, or four parents.

Anna, Brian, Rachel, and Ken get along real well with some of their parents, not so well with others. This has more to do with the parents' choices than if there's a "step" in their name.

The four kids in this book are kids who love God and who live in blended families. A blended family means the parents have divorced and at least one parent has married another person who may or may not have kids. Anna, Brian, Rachel, and Ken have different family experiences but have discovered three important truths: (1) divorce is hard; (2) you can make happiness in a blended family; (3) God is the only one who can give security during divorce and new family blending. We've asked them to introduce themselves and tell you their stories in this book.

I'm Anna and I have four parents, two sisters, a half-brother, and a half-sister. "Half" means they're my dad's kids, but not my mom's; they'd be "step" if they were neither my dad's or mom's kids but my dad or mom became their parent through marriage.

My stepdad married my mom and now lives with us and my two sisters. I see my dad, stepmom, and their two kids every other weekend, sometimes more.

I like to play piano and watch basketball. My friends say they like my smile. I'm really active in my church group. When I get older I want to go on our church's mission trips—you have to be in ninth grade to do that. But I can do other neat stuff like teach in Bible school. I was really nervous the first time I taught. I thought my nervousness meant I didn't have enough faith, but my leader said being nervous can mean you take the job seriously. Bible school went great, and I was glad I didn't back out. For a long time, I've wanted to be a teacher. I'm glad God gives me chances to learn how to be one. I love little kids.

I'm Rachel. The three things I like about myself are my naturally curly brown hair, my blue eyes, and my sense of humor. I'm shy at first, and then I talk so much you can't get a word in edgewise.

I live with my dad, stepmom, a stepsister and two half-brothers. My mom never remarried. Some people think it's strange that I'm a girl and I live with my dad. But that's the way it's been for as long as I can remember, so it seems normal to me. I'm glad God gave me my dad and stepmom. I don't see my mom much. She used to come for a week in summer, but she hasn't done that for a while.

I play in band at school. I like to make people happy by smiling at them or becoming friends with them. I also like to make people proud of me. I'm pretty laid back. One thing you might think strange is that I love cows—I mean people take cows for granted. Just think of all the stuff they give us: milk, cheese, butter, something pretty to look at when you're driving. People think they're stupid animals, but they're wrong.

I'm Ken. I hate animal abuse. Some experimentation is okay, because if they hadn't tried medicines on animals first, most of us wouldn't be alive today. But trying make-up and doing painful experiments on animals is stupid. Who needs make-up anyway?

I live with my dad and stepmom. My mom married a different husband, and they live about an hour away. I see them most weekends, and I can call anytime. My stepdad had one kid when they married, and he's about my age. Then he and my mom had a son who's about two now.

I go to Morgan Middle School and make good grades (is that bragging?). I think making good grades is important because it means I can get into a better college and have more jobs to choose from. I go to church on Sundays and Wednesdays, and I try to make God happy by the way I act every day. I'm the only boy in my Sunday school class, but I don't mind because there are lots of guys a year older or younger.

I'm Brian. I like all kinds of sports. This year I play basketball and baseball. My favorite subject is math. It's really fun. I have brown hair and hazel eyes.

My parents divorced when I was three, so I don't remember much about it. I live with my mom and stepdad, their daughter, and my older brother. My dad married Paula, and they stayed married a year, got divorced, remarried, and then divorced again. A few years later my dad met my current stepmom, and they've been married about five years.

Introduction

I see my dad every other weekend, and he comes to all my ball games. When I'm at his house, I sleep in a big bedroom with my stepbrothers or I sleep in the living room. Home is where my mom and stepdad are. I go to church here, school here, everything here. In fact, even when I'm at my dad's for the weekend, he brings me back for school and church events.

 You and Me

1. We've introduced ourselves to you. What are you like? What do you like to do? Who are your favorite people? What is your blended family like?

2. What makes each of your parents easy to get along with? Hard? How do you see God in them? How do they see God in you by the way you treat them?

3. What do you do to make yourself easy to get along with?
   - express emotions calmly
   - listen to my parents' opinions
   - explain why I feel as I do
   - understand why others feel as they do
   - enjoy being with my family
   - speak with kindness even when I feel cross
   - treat sisters and brothers well
   - Be happy with those who are happy and weep with those who weep (Romans 12:15)

1

Memories and Feelings

My parents divorced when I was seven," said Anna. "It was hot when they separated, so it must have been summer. But they didn't divorce until March. Divorces must take a long time. My mom's second marriage was a year later. They didn't stay married long. Then she married my current stepdad."

"My dad got married four times, twice to the same person," said Brian.

"Some friends think parents are careless to marry so many people. It makes me feel bad when they say that. I think my mom just had bad luck," said Anna.

"I know," said Rachel. "But parents make mistakes too. I think a lot of it has to do with thinking you don't deserve better, so you settle for less than the best for you. My mom actually told my dad that he'd never get anybody better than her. He believed her and married her. I came along, and then Mom left."

"That's terrible!" sympathized Anna.

"Yeah," agreed Rachel. "I know it's not my fault, but I can't help feeling that if I'd been better in some way, they wouldn't have divorced."

"For me the divorce wasn't nearly as bad as the remarriage," said Brian. "When my dad started seeing the woman who became my stepmom, I didn't like her because she took time away from my dad and me. My dad and I are great friends as well as father and son. I like my stepmom now, but it took a while."

"I had a tough time liking my stepparent too, but for a different reason," said Rachel. "When Dad and my stepmom married, I worried that their marriage would end up in divorce like my mom's and dad's. It took a long time to grow close to my stepmom. I didn't want to love her in case she didn't stay."

"When my mom and stepdad married, we moved to a new house. My grandfather, who had been living with us, moved to an apartment," explained Anna. "He hadn't wanted my mom to marry my stepdad. About three months later he died. My sister Lindsay was crushed! We all were, but she was especially close to Grandfather and never got over it. She feels our stepdad killed Grandfather, because he had to move out when our stepdad moved in."

"That must have been awful," said Ken.

"It was and is," said Anna. "It's made things really tense. I keep praying it will get better."

"I don't remember much about my parents' divorce or my dad's remarriage," said Ken. "He's been married to my stepmom for about nine years, and I've lived with them all that time, so it seems like home with her. She gives me permission and advice just like a regular parent. And like a regular parent, she likes to bug me. The other day she was acting crazy with a shampoo bottle. It was funny."

"I understand that my parents got divorced for the better. They fought a lot before they divorced," said Anna, "so things are much better in that respect. Also, my dad and stepmom have a little girl who is almost four and a little boy who is one. I love them so much. I feel as if they are my own brother and sister. If my parents had not gotten divorced I would never have had them."

"I bet it's easy to like them because they're little," said Ken. "My stepbrother and half-brother get on my nerves. They're pretty bratty. They argue about everything and get their way. Unfortunately my stepmom gives in to them."

"What do you do?" asked Anna.

"I kind of ignore them," said Ken. "Because I'm older I can basically do whatever I want. They don't argue much with me."

"Maybe that's one good thing about your blended family," suggested Brian. "You can help those kids learn to cooperate."

"Maybe," said Ken.

"I wish my parents hadn't divorced, but I'm glad I still have two parents," said Brian. "My dad and I are so much alike personality-wise and physically that I wouldn't want to lose him. He's always been involved in my life. We talk a lot in the car on the way to or from his house. He comes to every ball game I have."

"My dad doesn't do stuff like that with me," said Anna, "but I know he loves me. He tells everybody what I make on my report card. His friends see me and say, 'Your dad told me you got three A's!' Sometimes his bragging annoys me, but I guess that's his way of showing me he's proud of me and he loves me."

"Being in a blended family is nice because we're never lonely," said Rachel. "Because our family is so big, there's always somebody around to talk to or do things with."

"It's funny though," said Brian. "Sometimes I still get lonely for my other parent, no matter how big my family is. When my parents divorced, I was young and didn't think much about it. I just knew my dad would be there every other weekend. But now I think more about it. When I was eleven I decided I wanted to live with my dad. I'm not really sure why. Every night at bedtime I'd started crying and say, 'I want to live with Dad.' I guess I was just lonely for him."

"I like living with my dad and stepmom," said Ken. "But in the summer when I live with my mom, her place starts feeling like home. No matter which place I live, I feel a little homesick for the other place."

"That must mean you like both places," suggested Anna.

"I guess so," said Ken. "I never thought of that."

"Sometimes my mom gets jealous because my dad makes more money than she does and that gives him more freedom," said Brian. "He bought a new car recently, and I talked a lot about it. When I saw her get jealous I talked less."

"I hear my parents talk about finances and insurance and that kind of stuff. They get kind of worried sounding," said Rachel.

"One thing I don't like is when my parents try to talk through me," said Ken. " 'What does your mother think about this?' or 'What did Dad say about that?' I want them just to talk to each other."

"Me too. But I guess if they could do that, they'd still be married," said Brian. "Sometimes when I tell my friends my parents divorced and remarried they say 'I'm sorry.' That comes across strange. My friends can't do much about it."

"What do you want them to say?" said Anna.

"I don't know," said Brian. "I guess just listen, and not get all weird."

"I just want us to be friends and have fun together," said Rachel.

"Yeah, my friends are one of the ways God gives me happiness," said Anna. "We don't always have to talk about sad things or hard things. We can just be friends."

 ## *You and Me*

1. Being in a blended family brings us lots of feelings: sadness, love, anger, fear, wonder, worries, confusion, hope. When have you had these feelings? What do you do about these feelings?

2. What do you remember about your parents' divorce? Remarriage? What was easy and hard? What questions do you still have? Whom will you ask?

3. People who study stepfamilies say it takes an average of five years for a family to feel blended. How have you seen this in your family?

4. How have things changed (improved or gotten worse) since those early days? How does God help you with the hard things? Encourage you to focus on the good?

2

Sad Times

Being in a blended family can give you some strange problems," said Anna. "When my stepmom gives me clothes for birthday or Christmas, I have to give them back to her after I outgrow them for her daughter to use. Since she gave them to me as a present, I think I should get to keep them—maybe for my kids."

"When I get a bad grade or do something bad I get two lectures," said Brian.

"And it can be hard deciding where to spend holidays," said Ken.

"Having more parents makes things more complicated. My sister blames the remarriage for Grandfather's death, so she acts mean and hateful. My other sister just gets quiet when the arguments start. Our stepdad won't put up with either hatefulness or quietness. He yells at Lindsay and tells Leslee to wipe the smug expression off her face. That gets everybody fighting."

"I don't see what's wrong with just being quiet. And I can see why Lindsay would be upset, even though she doesn't say it the best way," said Rachel.

"Yeah, she misses my grandfather a lot," said Anna. "I wish

my family could understand each other rather than fight all the time. If I see why Lindsay feels the way she does, why don't my mom and stepdad? And if Leslee would rather be quiet than say something she regrets, why can't that be okay?"

"That makes sense to me. When my family fights, I feel awful," said Ken. "After my dad and stepmom married, my grades fell for about a year. I was sad a lot. Things got gradually better, but it was awful for a while."

"During fights I get to feeling like our whole family is going to fall apart," said Anna. "I feel like I can't do anything right. I wish things would get better."

"Me too," said Rachel. "My mom's not around, and just thinking about her gets me all upset. I wonder why she left and why she won't come see me."

"That's her problem, not yours," said Brian. "She doesn't know how to love."

"I know, I know," said Rachel. "But what do you do with the hurt?"

"I lean really hard on God," said Anna. "First I just feel sad for a while. Then I talk to God or write down my feelings. I write tons of angry letters. Most of the time I tear them up."

"I like to write songs," said Ken. "I write my best stuff when I'm sad."

"When I get really mad, I lift weights or shoot baskets," said Brian. "If I don't get active, I put my fist through the wall. That doesn't go over very well."

"I take walks," said Rachel. "I used to be afraid to talk to God about my anger, 'cause I figured He didn't approve. But since God knows I feel this way, I might as well tell Him about it. He helps me get the anger out and feel better."

"I'm so glad God understands us," said Anna. "But it's still hard."

"Yes, it is," agreed Ken. "And it takes time. Things are really calm at my house now, but it wasn't always that way."

"It's funny the things that get you," said Anna. "One day my sister was upset about something at school. She'd been crying, and my stepdad got mad about dishes in the dishwasher. I couldn't take anymore. I jumped up and exploded. Here my sister was hurting and he yelled at her about some dumb dishes. I felt he was insensitive and I said so!"

"Did you get in trouble?" asked Rachel.

"Yeah, but it was almost worth it," said Anna sheepishly. "I just had to say how I felt."

"It's hard to know when to talk and when to keep quiet," agreed Brian. "Like when my dad won't be real honest with my stepmom about how he feels."

"Do you say anything?" asked Rachel.

"When we're by ourselves I do. I say, 'Are you sure? Wouldn't it be better to talk it out rather than just give in?' " said Brian. "My dad and I understand each other because we're men. I don't like the way she bosses him around."

"My dad and I understand each other too," said Rachel. "But I'm no man!"

"Maybe it has more to do with personality," suggested Ken.

"I think it does," agreed Anna. "My dad has never been

good at being a dad. He yells over dumb stuff, like if my stepmom's late or I can't find the hammer. He has the same problems with my half-brother, so it's not a guy/girl thing."

"You must really hate your dad," said Rachel.

"No, I really don't," said Anna. "I love him a lot, and he loves me. He has good qualities. He just blows things out of proportion. He didn't grow up in a loving family, so he has a lot to overcome."

"My parents don't yell at each other or anything like that, but it's hard to go back and forth between houses," said Ken. "With my dad and stepmom, things are uniform and everything has a place and time. At my mom's, things are more relaxed."

"Sometimes I wish my family were normal: a mom, a dad, two kids. We would go places together, do things on weekends, and go to church on Sundays. When you have four parents, you have to work harder to please everyone," said Anna.

"Yeah," said Ken. "But in another sense my family with four parents is like a family with two parents. We all have problems. And we've all got to listen to God for help in solving them."

 You and Me

1. We've told you about some of our sad times. What sad times do you have? Who in your family seems to feel this

sadness most openly? Who seems to feel it without saying much? Which of these actions help you through your sad and mad times?

- Write it down
- Talk to the parent I'm upset with
- Talk to a different parent
- Listen to Christian music
- Talk to a friend
- Talk to God
- Read your Bible
- Remember favorite Bible verses
- Understand why adults act as they do
- Think about happy times

2. God likes some things that happen in your family and doesn't like other things. But He loves you and takes care of you through all of them. Psalm 121 says God will care for you through all situations. How does God "help"? not "let your foot slip"? "watch over you"? "keep you from all harm"? "watch over your coming and going"?

Philippians 4:19 says, "My God will meet all your needs." How has God helped you through an unfair or sad circumstance in your family?

3. We can't solve every problem in our families. That's because our parents make some choices that have nothing to do with us. But we can learn from our parents' mistakes. What do your parents do that you want to repeat in your own marriage and parenting? What do you want to change? God will help.

3

Happy Times

There are lots of good things about living in my blended family. In fact I can't think of anything really bad at my house. It's just like a normal home. My stepdad's just like a parent. I can honestly say I have three parents. My stepdad doesn't take my dad's place, but he loves me and takes care of me," said Brian.

"What about your stepmom?" said Anna.

"She still feels like a stepmom," said Brian.

"My stepdad feels like a stepdad—an extra adult I happen to know," said Ken. "But my stepmom feels like a mom. Maybe because I'm with her more."

"Some of the stuff that happens in blended families is normal stuff," explained Brian. "At my mom's house, the place I call home, I like to stay in my room a lot. My mom keeps asking what's wrong. I just want to be alone to think, that's all. I listen to the radio, do homework, stuff like that. My mom gets on my nerves when she keeps asking. But stuff like that happens in every family."

"Yeah, I like the regular stuff," said Anna. "My dad is really protective."

"My stepmom is so cool," said Rachel. "She's a great cook

and will listen to me. She tells me how she handled things when she was a kid. She really understands, really knows how it feels. She does get mad about things, but I guess everybody does that sometimes."

"My mom is great too," said Anna. "I can't tell how many times she's saved me. Once I needed a costume for a school play and I forgot to tell her. She stayed up all night making it and didn't get mad. Also, and this may sound really weird, she can really pack a suitcase. She always puts in just the things I need and want when I go to camp or somewhere like that. She knows what I like, and I love to go shopping with her. We're really close."

"One thing I like about our family is we can all laugh together," said Ken. "When one person is in a bad mood, the others cheer him up."

"My dad's not real good at laughing and stuff like that," said Anna. "He doesn't listen very well either. But he does a lot of good things, and he's getting better at the listening part. Last night when we talked, we really seemed to understand each other. It was great."

"One good thing I can say about my stepmom is that she and my dad really know how to have fun," said Brian.

"My dad and stepmom are happy together," said Rachel. "Their relationship seems pretty good to me. Sometimes they argue, especially if one is tired or sad, but most of the time things are on a pretty even keel."

"I wish it were that way at my house," said Anna. "But my sisters and I get along really well. And my friends are great."

"I'm still me no matter what my family is like," said Brian. "It does get kinda complicated when something is going on at my mom's, and it's supposed to be my weekend with my dad. Most of the time Dad is happy to take me though, even if it's a long drive."

"Or I just trade weekends," said Ken. "Usually that works out."

"There are a few advantages to having four parents. You get double birthday, so more presents," said Brian. "And when one Christmas is over, there's still another to look forward to."

"We have to travel a lot to get both places on the same day or the same weekend," said Ken. "Or sometimes we switch. Like for Easter we go to my mom's parents one time and to my grandparents on my dad's side the next."

"And no matter what our family situation, God always takes care of us. Even when a parent doesn't care or doesn't treat you right, God is there to give you security and love," said Anna.

"Yeah, being in a blended family is sort of like having hazel eyes," said Brian. "Some people have it, some don't. We still can do good, be smart, have fun."

 ## *You and Me*

1. What do you like about your mom? stepmom? dad? stepdad?

2. What's normal about your family? What's happy about your family?

3. Happiness is something to which all family members contribute. What actions do you take to bring happiness in your family?
- Listen
- Sincerely compliment other family members
- Share dreams
- Show interest in parents, brothers, sisters
- Tell about your day
- Go places together
- Don't do all the talking
- Don't do all the listening
- Show kindness even when you don't feel like it
- Tell about good or funny things family members have done
- Try to understand mean actions rather than automatically react

4

God Then, Now, and in My Future

God makes a big difference in my family happiness," said Brian. "I remember coming home from school when I was in sixth grade really upset. I burst out crying and then asked God for peace. I just felt so calm. Now whenever I get uptight about anything, I ask God to calm me down."

"Yeah, it seems easier to handle everything with God," said Ken.

"Sometimes I don't do right with my praying, though," admitted Brian. "Like for awhile at school I hadn't been getting my homework. I'd pray, 'Do something God, please!' and the teacher would put off turning in that assignment or say we could turn it in late for ten percent off. That kind of praying won't work forever."

"That's kinda like using God, not loving Him," said Rachel.

"God's not just for the bad times. He makes the happy times happier too," added Anna. "I love church, even though none of my parents go. I wish they went. My dad thinks church is dumb. He doesn't want to depend on anyone. Sometimes he criticizes me because I go to church. I wish he understood."

"I wish he did too," said Brian. "All four of my parents have been in church as long as I can remember. I've probably been going since before I was born."

"How'd you get in church, Anna, if your parents don't go?" asked Ken.

"My friend Amy invited me," said Anna. "We went to the same school. Now I go to a different school, but we're still great friends."

"My dad and stepmom are Christians and have been since they were my age," said Ken. "I've always known about and loved Jesus, but I made my commitment public last year. My parents trust me because they know I'm a Christian and I won't do anything God would not want me to do."

"My dad's a strong Christian," said Rachel. "My stepmom goes to church, but I don't know if she's a Christian yet. She doesn't say much about God. I became a Christian when I was eight. I like knowing Jesus cares and has written me a letter called the Bible. I like the verse that says God knows everything I've been through, all my pain. It reminds me He's not far from me."

"Yeah, sometimes I do feel like God is far away," agreed Anna. "But He's not. Psalm 139 is my favorite chapter. It says something like 'Search me, Lord. You created me, You know my every thought and feeling, You knit me together in my mother's womb.' That last part is my favorite because it shows I'm not junk."

"My favorite Bible verse is 'Do unto others as you would have them do unto you,'" said Brian. "I'm usually a pretty nice guy to everybody, because I have no reason to be mean. Unless somebody's rude—then I tend to be rude."

"I like the verse about a friend sticking closer than a brother," said Ken.

"Yeah. Church is where my best friends are. Amy, Tamika, and I are almost inseparable," said Anna. "When they're around I never feel ugly or lonely."

"When sad things happen, our group of friends at church helps each other through. Melody has been through divorce and remarriage too. She's a real inspiration to me," said Rachel. "Mason's dad had an operation. And we were all excited when Barry made the track team. Good or bad, we do it together."

"But God doesn't stay at church," said Anna. "He goes with me to school. He gives me the courage to make new friends."

"God keeps me from cheating and reminds me to be honest when it would be easier to lie," said Rachel. "I want people to know they can trust me."

"And God helps me keep my cool in sports," said Brian. "Sometimes I have a really bad temper. God helps me with my temper at home too."

"God is always there for me. Even though my mom left, God will never divorce me," said Rachel.

"I'm counting on God to help me know how to love. Love confuses me," said Anna. "I think a lot of kids with divorced parents wonder what love is. I do. I don't understand how people are married until they die. I've never had that. Some of my friends' parents have always been married, and it's so weird to me."

"My friend's dad and stepmom are getting divorced," said Ken. "Though things seem pretty secure at my house, I wonder if divorce will happen again."

"I know what it's like to love a parent, sister, or friend, but what is it like to love a spouse for a lifetime?" asked Anna. "Each time my mom got married, she committed to love the man she married for life. But twice she divorced. Why?"

"Sometimes I wonder if I'll ever have love," said Rachel. "I'm scared to get into a relationship because I never want to get divorced."

"I guess in a way that's good because we'll work harder on marriage," said Anna. "I know that love takes work, and I won't take it for granted. I'll also watch carefully the kind of person I pick to marry. My youth leader said her parents didn't get along very well, and she had to work extra hard to build a good marriage. But she's succeeding. They're going on seventeen years now."

"My girlfriend and I have been dating for eight months," said Brian. "We get along great. The only thing that worries me is she can be really mean. She's never mean to me though."

"But couldn't she get mean if you married her?" said Anna. "Maybe she's just on her good behavior to impress you. I've heard you have to watch how a person treats everybody, not just you."

"I don't think she'd ever treat me badly," said Brian.

"Anna may be right," said Ken. "My dad says my mom never raised her voice at him until about a year after they married. Then the yelling was awful. Looking back, he remembers that she used to yell at other people that way."

"My stepmom says love is something you choose, not something that happens or doesn't happen," said Rachel. "She always says, 'Choose to be kind, Rachel.'"

"If my parents had just been nice to each other in the first place, their love would have lasted. They wouldn't have divorced," said Anna. "I'm going to choose to be kind no matter how grouchy I feel. God is teaching me how."

"I'm going to learn from my parents' mistakes," said Ken. "I know they made some wrong choices and do a lot of wrong things. But I don't hate them for what they've done. I know I'll be tempted to make the same mistakes because that's what I grew up with. But with God's help I'll change."

"I know I can create a loving home and be a loving parent," said Rachel.

"Me too. I'm going to be careful about who I marry," said Ken. "Unless I see the girl God has for me, I'm just going to wait. Too many people don't wait. They take the first person who comes along."

"The Bible says we've got to love others as we love ourselves," said Brian. "If we don't like ourselves, we can't love others very well."

"And if we don't believe we deserve a good marriage, we may not make one," said Anna. "I'm going to build a happy family because God made me good."

"I'm not going to get married early like my parents," said Brian. "My brother and his girlfriend have dated a year, and I can tell my parents are worried."

"I'm going to make sure I only date Christians," said Ken. "Then I won't find myself in love with a non-Christian."

"But just being a Christian isn't enough," said Brian. "Both my parents were Christians when they married, and they divorced."

"Well, yeah, but being a Christian is the first qualification on the list. Then I'll look for someone nice, someone I can talk to, and get along with," said Ken.

"Before I get married, I'm going to get a college education," said Anna. "Nobody in my family graduated from college except for one cousin. So I'm planning on being one of the first ones to graduate. I want to be a teacher."

"And I want to be an author-illustrator," said Rachel.

"I don't really care what I do, but I want to enjoy my work," said Brian.

"I want to be happy and help others be happy, married or not," said Ken.

 ## *You and Me*

1. What is your favorite Bible verse and why do you like it?

2. People who are already happy when they marry tend to create happy marriages. We're committed to make happiness by obeying God, treating people kindly, and choosing interesting jobs. How will these commitments help you create happiness before you marry? after you marry and have kids? What else will help?

3. Anna is right: It's hard to know lifetime love if you've never experienced it. Kids whose parents have divorced are more likely to divorce. But lifetime love is still possible with deliberate work. Love is a commitment, a decision, a choice. Whom do you know who has been married several years and is still in love? How do they live out their love commitment? How can you imitate their love?

5

Our Advice to You

If your family is going through divorce, find somebody to talk to," said Brian. "When you're all jumbled up inside, you need an outlet. Right now, my person is my mom. Your person might be your parents, a grandparent, a teacher, an adult at church. Just be sure to find somebody. God will give you someone."

"Sometimes I talk to friends," said Ken. "They don't always believe things are as bad as they are. They say, 'That's normal.' But it's not normal for two people who loved each other once not to love each other now. And it's not normal for two people to fight a lot. But since I can't change it, I do the best I can."

"Don't blame yourself for your parents' divorce," said Rachel. "It's not your fault that your parents have divorced and remarried. You had nothing to do with their decision. They divorced because of problems they were unable to resolve in their relationship. It's not something to do with you or the way you acted."

"It's hard to believe, but even parents have a lot of problems," said Anna. "Especially when you're really small, you think parents are perfect. They're not. They make bad choices and do dumb things—sometimes that leads to divorce."

"Parents worry about the divorce too. They have a lot of sadness about it," said Rachel. "They worry about how it will affect you."

"They also worry about how they'll do things alone that they did together before—like pay the bills and make decisions," said Ken.

"And somebody has to move out and get another place to live," said Brian.

"When you're going through all this, it's a big help to turn to Jesus," said Anna. "He knows exactly what you're going through. He knows your anger, your sadness, your fear. Pray hard for guidance and read your Bible. It's a wonderful message from God."

"No matter how hard things seem to be, you'll get through it," assured Brian. "Keep the communication open between you and God, and between you and your parents. It will make things easier for all of you."

"Then be happy when things go well," added Rachel. "And remember that God will never divorce you."

You and Me

1. We've given you our advice. What advice would you give to someone living in a blended family? What do you know now that wish you had known earlier?

2. Many things can change, but one thing never changes: God always loves you and is always there for you. God won't divorce you, move away from you, or hurt you. He will always understand you, stay with you, help you, teach you. How have you experienced this security? How does it show in your life?

3. One of the neatest ways God loves us is by giving us people who love us. These include parents, stepparents, siblings, teachers, and friends. Through what people does God love you? How does God love people through you?

6

Other Friends Who Can Help

If you live in a blended family or know someone who does, these sources can help you build happiness in your family, answer your questions, or direct you to more help.

- Make friends with other families and stepfamilies. Look around for other blended families in your church. Choose one or two that seem very happy together. Watch and imitate the good things they do. Ask their secrets to happiness. Join a stepfamilies support group. All families can encourage each other.

- Read the Bible and read Christian books. The Bible and books like *Family Survival Guide* (Victor Books, 1825 College Avenue, Wheaton, IL 60187) offer tips for getting along in your family, whether blended or not.

- Keep a journal by writing your feelings and experiences every day or two. Notice how God heals you and brings joy in your family. *My Parents Got a Divorce* by Gary Sprague (Chariot Family Publishing, 20 Lincoln Avenue, Elgin, IL 60120) offers sample experiences and feelings you might want to write about. In this book Christian kids tell how they moved from hurt to hope.

• Find information. The Stepfamily Association of America, 215 Centennial Mall South, Suite 212, Lincoln, NE 68508. 1-800-735-0329 provides support and education for stepfamilies. Their newsletter, called *Stepfamilies*, offers relationship tips, problem solving strategies, books and resources, research, and letters from other stepfamilies. The association also offers books, membership, and support groups. To order information or find out a support group in your area, dial the above toll free number or write to the address.

❖ PARENTS ❖

Are you looking for fun ways to bring the Bible to life in the lives of your children?

Chariot Family Publishing has hundreds of books, toys, games, and videos that help teach your children the Bible and apply it to their everyday lives.

Look for these educational, inspirational, and fun products at your local Christian bookstore.